Does Love Come Back?

Rewa Z.

BookLeaf
Publishing

India | USA | UK

Made with ❤ on the BookLeaf Publishing Platform

www.bookleafpub.in

www.bookleafpub.com

Dedication

To the person who has been my home in every sense of the word and to those whose support has carried me through every page.

Preface

I was in seventh grade when I first started writing poems. Back then, it was all about making them rhyme. Gradually, I began expressing myself and pouring my heart and soul into everything I wrote. Since 2012, I've written around 200 poems, both short and long, in English, Hindi, and Marathi. I've also written a few *shayaris* and tried my hand at simple French poems.

In this life, I have fallen in love with writing, staring at pretty skies, telling the moon how beautiful it looks, sitting by the sea, and letting my soul soak in the serenity.

A little about this book:
It's a love story divided into chapters. A story of how two people are never truly equal, yet love binds them together.
It's about acceptance, faith, patience, and hope.

Acknowledgements

Thanks to all who have played a part, however small, in making this work possible.

Chapter 1.

The beginning: One of a kind

The night before was rather stormy.
The next morning, as I sat in the park, sipping coffee, I
looked beside me.
And there it was, that dreamy smile of yours.
You stared at me as if in your mind,
we were eighty, married, and carrying with us a lifetime
of love.

Back to reality.

We weren't more than friends.
Yet, I sensed something dawning on me.
A little ray of sunshine made its way through the clouds.
I felt the silence around and chaos within, and you
sensed it too,
so you pulled me a little closer
and told me what you ought to.
That moment, right there, was a confession of love
and a promise of a lifelong friendship.

Chapter 1.
The beginning: One of a kind

I remember spending the whole day
laughing and giggling as if life was perfect.
That evening, though the sun was setting,
I could still feel the warmth of our friendship.
I could feel the butterflies in my stomach
and love growing within me.
It felt as if that evening,
the sky was painting our love story
in the most beautiful shades I'd ever seen.
When, finally, the sun had set on my loneliness,
it left behind a gift in the form of
the most beautiful person I had ever seen
and the warmest soul I had ever met—
a person I could call Love,
a person I could finally call mine.

Chapter 1.

The beginning: One of a kind

The night fell upon me like a gentle breeze.
Back home, I stood in front of the mirror
and saw you looking at me.
You held my hand in silence
and the touch told me everything,
sounds of breath and heartbeats—
beautiful, intense, and sweet.
The moon shone in your eyes,
and the stars sparkled in mine,
for when I dreamt that night
everything was about us.

Chapter 2.

The mask, the unmasking

But love isn't perfect, is it?
There are masks we all hide behind.

Oh, how I wish I could show you my fears
and introduce you to the insecurities I've gathered over
the years.
Tell you how they keep me up at night,
show you how each day I put up a fight
against these thoughts that come in as guests
and stay as if they own the place,
catch me in my own mind while I try to escape,
choke me, hurt me, and leave me hopeless.

But then I saw you walking towards me,
the only one who accepted me with all my flaws.
Oh dear, how could I dare deceive you more?
A faulty piece still has to work, one way or the other.

Chapter 2.

The mask, the unmasking

Our memories are crystal clear in my mind.
I remember that one day
when you saw me staring blankly at the sky.
It felt as if you could hear me scream inside.
When you gently, playfully patted my head,
you held me without holding me and saved me
unknowingly.
That warm touch pulled me out of my evil thoughts
before they could consume me, and within no time,
I found myself smiling again.

The mask was coming off, and as much nervous as I was,
I knew I had found a companion I once wished for.

Chapter 2.

The mask, the unmasking

All I needed was courage.
The courage to confess my insecurities and fears.
But my eyes spoke louder, and you heard me.

So every time we went out,
you sowed the seeds of self-love,
so that no one could ever bog me down.

You made me strong.
Strong, with or without you.

All I had asked from life was a person who loved me.
Life blessed me with an angel,
and I couldn't be more grateful.

Chapter 3.

From 'love' to 'Love'

Love walked in when I was alone.
Love held my hand and took me onto a path unknown,
showed me how little I'd known myself,
read me like a story,
kept me from spiraling when he saw my fears rushing in,
stayed with me until I could breathe again,
told me about things I had never heard of,
and carved them in places I was conscious of.

Love was the dream I thought would never come true.

Chapter 3.

From 'love' to 'Love'

When Love chose me,
he chose me with all my flaws.
He welcomed my insecurities; he was kind to them.
Love knew how beautiful I would look without them.
So Love kissed them away, one at a time.
He knew he had to take down the walls and armors
that masked my vulnerability,
but Love didn't break them.
He melted them with kindness and patience.
He saw the little girl inside the walls,
sitting in a corner she named "unknown."
And Love offered her his hand.
Love offered me himself.
He stayed, he sheltered, and he showed me
how to love myself once again.

Chapter 3.

From 'love' to 'Love'

He made it look effortless.
He made it look effortless
when he planned the entire day.
He made it look effortless when he bought a birthday gift
after planning it for an entire month.
He made it look effortless when he answered my calls
and eased my anxiety with his patience and calm;
Love brought back my smile as if it were never lost.
He made it look effortless when he said he knew why I
was upset,
but in his head he had thought of a hundred things that
could have been wrong.
He made it look effortless
when he opened up about his fears,
while in his mind he was still anxious.
He made it look effortless
when he did all that he did for me.
I can only imagine the strength and patience
of the person who loves for all that I am.

Chapter 3.
From 'love' to 'Love'

Life isn't perfect, and neither is love.
So when life took an unexpected turn,
I thought I was holding on tightly to Love.
But it wasn't him; it was the strength within.

When you're strong for someone else, when you keep
giving,
you forget the importance of receiving.
Love became a part of me, until one day,
Love had to leave.
Because Love wanted to be perfect,
but Love didn't like himself.
Love didn't let me love him the way he did.
Strong, patient, kind, gentle, and everything else that
Love was to me,
he couldn't be the same to himself.
Neither did he want to give me a chance.
Some stories are beautiful,
yet they end up as scars.

Chapter 4.

Love came, Love left

You left before I could tell you what you deserved.
You disappeared before I could show you my world.
Vanished from my sight, just when I wanted to look at
you all my life,
taking me away in pieces
every time you joked about leaving.
Took me away in a breath,
when you vanished to never return.
I stood still as if
I'd just stepped into a world I'd never known.
The walls of my home were muted peach,
the couch you held me on was beige.
The bookshelf was filled with comics and mysteries,
how I had forgotten what home looked like after I found
mine in your eyes.
The only thing I remember was a purple dreamcatcher.
I wonder why it didn't work,
when all it had to do was filter the nightmares.
I wonder if it was all a dream from the beginning,
and I had just woken up to reality.

Chapter 4.

Love came, Love left

I was there, existing like words scattered everywhere.
Love made me the story that I am today.
He was the beginning and the end.
He walked in as a guest, made me his friend,
then became one with my mind and soul.

I can still feel his hands holding mine,
his lips on my cheeks, and on all the places
he told me were beautiful.

I still look back to reminisce
about his words, his voice, his eyes,
and the moments when time stood still.

Chapter 5.

Little things

I found you in the little things.
I found you in your everyday routine —
when you casually hummed the songs you liked,
when you smiled like a kid
as you saw me through the window,
when you slipped an extra packet of chips into the cart,
and did the smallest things that made me laugh.
How could I not be obsessed with a person
who loved me unapologetically?

Chapter 5.

Little things

I found you in the playlists you made
and in the journals you maintained.
I found you when I couldn't take my eyes off you,
watching you laugh your heart out.
I found you in the letters you wrote
when we couldn't meet.
Who said old-school love was boring?
Before I realized it, we were right there.
Fancy dreams and expensive gifts never mattered.
Your hand in mine, the comfort in your voice,
your presence, and resting my head on your shoulder
were worth far more than roses and diamonds.
And there was nothing more I could have asked for.

Chapter 5.
Little things

How could little things not matter?
Aren't we all made of atoms, invisibly beautiful?
Who said gestures are synonymous with gifts?
I had mine standing right in front of me,
looking into my eyes
as if he saw his dreams through mine, shining bright.
And these little places turned into a void.
How could I fill them again?
Like flowers growing in the places you left,
they carried your scent.
And I've visited this garden of mine
and called it by your name — Love.

Chapter 6.
The journey ends: Solace within

I couldn't track time anymore.
I realized how we never had control
when hours passed by, staring blankly at the sky.
My heart still couldn't understand
whether you were truly gone
or still there, hiding somewhere.
I kept hoping and waiting for you to surprise me—
to change reality, to make it kinder to the part of me was
still waiting for you.

Chapter 6.
The journey ends: Solace within

My mind was playing tug-of-war.
On one side, it tried to accept your absence;
on the other, it secretly manifested your presence.

Days passed by.

It was never about which side won—
it was about making peace with the fact
that reality had become hard to live with.

The only question I kept asking myself was,
"Will he ever return?"

Chapter 6.

The journey ends: Solace within

The rains silenced everything that night.
As I sat by the window, hoping you were there too,
looking at your photograph brought back a thousand
memories.
Just as I was about to put it back,
I looked at it one last time.
And then, the doorbell rang.
There you were, drenched and drained,
waiting for the same warmth
you once showered me with.
I couldn't be happier.
Love comes back when it's real.
It was now my turn to love you the way you did,
and in that moment, I promised myself to never let go of
you or us again.
That's where the journey finally came to an end.
All I could feel was love like never before,
and solace within.

So love comes back, right?
Well...

Chapter 7.

Does love come back?

True love sows the seeds of faith.
It takes roots, deep and strong,
growing quietly within, through heat and storms alike.
And one day, when hope feels like barren ground,
two tiny leaves emerge, shaped like a small green heart.
When you nurture true love, it returns,
and it returns stronger than ever.

Chapter 7.

Does love come back?

And now, when I look back,
I still fall for your smile,
the one I fell in love with years ago.

When we sat in the park, little did I know
that a love story could look this beautiful.

It begins with faith, respect, and kindness,
and ends with togetherness.

From unlearning ourselves to building a bond from the
ground up,
love has taught me to be patient,
and Love has taught me to hold his hand
and never let it go.

Chapter 7.

Does love come back?

So, does love come back?

When it's blue, pink, yellow, and green,
when it's all the shades your story has ever been,
when it's patient, slow, and steady,
when it's kind, when it's raw,
when it stays loyal through the ups and downs alike,
when it's roses and lilies,
and the mountains and the seas,
and when it's unconditional,
love comes back.